Gloucestershire & Somerset

Edited By Connor Matthews

First published in Great Britain in 2018 by:

Young Writers
Remus House
Coltsfoot Drive
Peterborough
PE2 9BF
Telephone: 01733 890066
Website: www.youngwriters.co.uk

All Rights Reserved
Book Design by Ashley Janson
© Copyright Contributors 2018
SB ISBN 978-1-78896-559-0
Printed and bound in the UK by BookPrintingUK
Website: www.bookprintinguk.com
YB0362J

FOREWORD

Young Writers was established in 1991, dedicated to encouraging reading and creative writing in young people. Our nationwide writing initiatives are designed to inspire ideas and give pupils the incentive to write, and in turn develop literacy skills and confidence, whilst participating in a fun, imaginative activity.

Few things are more encouraging for the aspiring writer than seeing their own work in print, so we are proud that our anthologies are able to give young authors this unique sense of confidence and pride in their abilities.

For our latest competition, Rhymecraft, primary school pupils were asked to enter a land of poetry where they used poetic techniques such as rhyme, simile and alliteration to bring their ideas to life. The result is an entertaining and imaginative anthology which will make a charming keepsake for years to come.

Each poem showcases the creativity and talent of these budding new writers as they learn the skills of writing, and we hope you are as entertained by them as we are.

CONTENTS

Independent Entries

Millie Castledine (9)	1
Millie Royce (10)	2
Mary Katie Nasilasila	5
Gracie May Wallis (10)	6
Elizabeth Downing (9)	8

Amberley Parochial School, Amberley

Arabella King (5)	10

Bishop Henderson CE Primary School, Taunton

Jack Tregunna (10)	11
Tomass Penny (10)	12
Tessa Burge (8)	13
Ethan Shuttleworth (8)	14
Lilianne Mariyam Liju (11)	15
Lydia Lambert (8)	16
Brayden Carl John Fitzgerald (8)	17
Esther Lambert (8)	18
Alexander James Coles (8)	19

Carrant Brook Junior School, Northway

Lachezar Petrov Genchev (9)	20
Lilly-Mae Lawrence (8)	21
Jaiden Maggs (10)	22
Niall Baker (11)	23
Drew Baker (9)	24
Ben Nicholls (8)	25
Emily Goodchild (8)	26
Zhaniyan Nikolov (10)	27

Combe Down CE Primary School, Combe Down

Mimi Colman-Deveney (11)	28

Exford CE First School, Exford

Tristan Graham (9)	29
Liam Callaert (8)	30
Emily Violet Illing (8)	31
Charlie Colin Glover (8)	32

Greatfield Park Primary School, Up Hatherley

Erin Summer Kay (7)	33
George Stone (7)	34

Hamp Academy, Bridgwater

Libby Boobyer (10)	35
Lewis Watts (10)	36
Mia Parker	37
Skye Godbeer	38
Connie Sara Valerie Downton (8)	39
Sophia Alcantara (9)	40
Ava Daniells (9)	41
Isobel Ferguson (9)	42

Haselbury Plucknett First School, Haselbury Plucknett

Evie John (8)	43

Hugh Sexey CE Middle School, Blackford

Daisy-Mae Suzie Valentine (9)	44

Huish Episcopi Primary School, Huish Episcopi

Janis Lusitis (11)	45
Lola James (10)	46
Euan Robertson (10)	47
Emma-Jane Keegan (10)	48
Matilda Valerie Stuckey (10)	49
Kyla Baker (10)	50
Ellis Beake (10)	51
Magnus Haines (10)	52
Uday Akshay Patel (9)	53
Hatty (11)	54
Kaia-Lara Hammond (11)	55
Alfie Cook (10)	56
Emily Anne Wheller (10)	57
Bella (10)	58
Jasmine (9)	59
Luke Padfield (10)	60
Samuel Lyes (11)	61

Moorlands Junior School, Bath

Livia Brain (10)	62

North Nibley CE Primary School, North Nibley

Abby Elizabeth Susan Hunter (8)	63
Joss Reynard (9)	64
Delphie Locke (9)	66
Amelie Ivy de Pass (8)	68
Beea Ward (7)	69
Emily Rea (8)	70
Nathan George Hunter (8)	71
Ollie Perry (8)	72
Olivia Prosser (8)	73
Jude James l'Anson (8)	74
Oliver Pitt (8)	75
Hannah Jade Stanulewicz (8)	76

Cara Sophia Saunderson (8)	77
Elliot Pretlove (7)	78
Ella Rose Thomson (9)	79
Grace Hall (7)	80
George Loveday (7)	81
Seb Bouvier (9)	82
Isabella Spiller (8)	83
Jacob Mydlowski (7)	84
Zak Lampard (8)	85
Freddy Romero-Brown (9)	86

Parkend Primary School, Parkend

Theia-Rose Williams (10)	87
Sonni Powell (7)	88
Brayden Powell (7)	89
Seth Waller (6)	90
Ella Jones (10)	91

St Mary's CE Primary School, Writhlington

Rhys Friend (8)	92
David Shave (7)	93
Hollie Davies (8)	94
Shylah (7)	95

St Michael's CE First School, Minehead

Ellie Sanderson (8)	96
Dylan Dean Newby (8)	97
Grace Hughes (8)	98
Sonny Newman (9)	99
Luca Gasperini (7)	100
Jade Clark (8)	101
Olivia Katie Glenn (9)	102
Ollu Rumbe (8)	103
Charlotte Cottington (8)	104
Eden Coley (9)	105
Lucie Matcham (9)	106
George Dalziel (8)	107
Evie James (8)	108
Chloe Chapman-Humfries (8)	109

Lexi H-A (8)	110
Darius Pranciskus Neverauskas (8)	111
George Andrew Hall (8)	112
Ava Butterworth (8)	113
Isla Sapsford (8)	114
Sophie Hilda Ross (8)	115
Christyanna Heath (9)	116
Eva Swinburn (8)	117
Aiden Fisher (9)	118
Ty Cooper (9)	119
Mya Ridehalgh (9)	120
Kelsey Clayton (9)	121
Sophie-Jo Morton-Watts (7)	122
Lenny Mark Morris (8)	123
Maddi Louise Clarke-Jennings (7)	124
Luke Brown (7)	125
Sid Jack Turner Williams (8)	126
Kaden Michael Owen (8)	127
David Bown (7)	128
Brendan Morley (9)	129
Isla May Helena Blustin (7)	130

Stow On The Wold Primary School, Stow On The Wold

Noah Perkins (7)	131
Ella White (7)	132
Alfie Marc Morris (8)	133
Caleb Austin Willoughby Harvey	134
Milah Valentine Keyte (7)	135
Darcey Sivalingam	136

Stroud And Cotswold Pupil Referral Services, Stroud

Peter Ind (10)	137
Blu Llewellyn (11)	138

The Richard Pate School, Cheltenham

Olivia Sophie Mourton (8)	139

Wellsprings Primary School, Taunton

Caleb Crook (7)	140
Theo Crook (7)	141
Raoul Parnici (8)	142
Charlotte Rawlings (7)	143
Tianna Frances Hathaway (8)	144
Jared Smale (8)	145
Angela Mackay (8)	146
Abigail Ralph (7)	147
Alexa Harris (7)	148
Mia Squire (7)	149
Emily Cross (7)	150
Lewis Horrobin (8)	151
Thomas Harriss (7)	152
Ollie Webber (8)	153
Alesha James (7)	154
Joshua Edward Comer (8)	155
Megan Chapman (8)	156
Elliot Barr (8)	157
Rosie Lynne Tiffany (7)	158
Hollie Jarman (8)	159
Mason Le Prevost (7)	160
Noah Derbe (7)	161
Richard Continho Leitao (7)	162
Theo Richie Hind (7)	163
Harry Woodland (8)	164

Westonbirt Prep School, Tetbury

Kacey Connolly (9)	165

THE POEMS

Could I Be?

Sometimes I sit there and wonder,
Just how life can be,
If I can be an astronaut,
Or a gymnast on TV.
Could I have a unicorn,
As white as the snow
And visit a land that I do not know
And let all my worries flutter away,
With nobody telling me what to do or say.

Millie Castledine (9)

The World Above

I took off the rocky edge,
And finished my ground pledge.
As I flew above the terrific, turquoise sea,
The mountain's gradient stared at me.
My dreams and goals were all complete,
I had nothing underneath my feet.

What is the world? Is it meant for fun?
What is the moon? What is the sun?
Are they just thoughts that don't exist?
Is it just another thing on my untrue list?

I soared into the magical sky,
Is the ground just a lie?
Why do some live down below?
There's a world above... don't you know?

Some dreams depend on love and hate,
While others are destined to be fate!
The part I play is the flying beast,
Every day I have a mixed animal feast.

While I fly I seem to think,
About all the colours I've seen like blue and pink.
Or maybe white and black,
Sometimes I turn round and go back.

I have no words for my feelings,
I say because I have no roofs or ceilings.

When I fly people stare,
Is it because I don't have much hair?
Or is it because I don't come in a pair.
I don't care what people think,
I refuse to be in a perfect sync.

I have to go down in the dark,
But I go back up when I see the sun's first spark.
When my adventure comes to a stop,
I have to go down I'm no longer top.

I can't fit in with the other birds,
They all have their own herds.

I have not a wife or any of my own kin,
People think I'm free but it's not quite a win.

I haven't got a song to make everything right,
I haven't got amazing eyes to soar through the night.
I haven't got a friend or two,
I can't carry a message through a simple *coo*.

The one thing I can do best,
Is flying up above the rest.

I have conquered my obstacles, ups and downs.
I have fought my fears and carried on through the frowns.
I have my possibilities my unfortunate events,
But these don't usually happen because I have more sense.

This adventure is soon to end,
But before I go round the last bend.
There's something that you should know,
Here it is, here I go...

You can reach your goals if you try,
For example me - now I can fly!

Millie Royce (10)

Phoenix Flame

Once again
Back again from edges end rise
Fiery phoenixes to a
New day begin

Shake the ash from your wing
Spread your lips and sing a soft
Sweet melody of eternal reign

For you are
King of yourself
And puppet to
No master.

Mary Katie Nasilasila

Lost

I feel lost,
Like a small boat lost at sea,
I see an island,
But the more I paddle,
The more I try,
The further away the island gets.

I see my friends and family,
Encouraging me to try,
I do, just for them,
But it doesn't make a difference,
I keep on getting sucked in,
Towards the darkness.

As time passes,
I lose my senses,
Everything turns black,
My head spins,
Up, down,
Left, right.

Then, suddenly,
I am locked in a small room,
I can see the key,
It is tied up high,
On a thin piece of string,
I reach, and fall.

Back again I go,
Into the world where no one knows,
I see visions,
Of people,
Strangers that I don't know,
Talking, about me.

They say I am troubled,
Deeply so,
A small round box is held by my mouth,
It goes into my mouth,
I swallow
And everything is clear.

Gracie May Wallis (10)

My World

This is a place where lions can roam,
That place would be a home.
Full of wild creatures tamed,
A lynx that is named...
Charlotte!
My chameleon that is named...
Scarlet!
They are both girls I know,
I've also got a marvellous monkey with a bow,
All of them are my friends,
All of them have each a separate den,
It's me who they love,
I've also got other animals
Including a dove,
Mammals, reptiles, birds
I all have,
I've got all of these including a phoenix
Called Gav,
One of the cats is as small as a baby,
The cat's fur is wavy.

Scarlet can wave with her tail.
Sorry, but I don't have an island whale.

Elizabeth Downing (9)

Fairy Land

In Fairyland,
It is as small as your hand,
Glittery colours all around,
Rainbows and clouds hear the sounds.
Princess Fairy has met a prince,
He is wearing a suit of sparkly chintz.
They are having a party in the hall,
You can come too, it will be a ball.

Arabella King (5)
Amberley Parochial School, Amberley

The Frosty Pirate Rules

Shiver my timbers, shiver my soul,
Finding treasures is our goal,
We're the pirates of Frosty Hollow,
We love sailing on our ship, Apollo.
Yo-ho, yo-ho, our secret lobby is a no-go zone,
All of the crew is here always,
My favourites, Old Pete and Captain Squid,
Who drink beer all day.
Ahoy there, me hearties,
The sea is close to freezing,
Unlucky for the puny pirates about to walk the plank
Who are pleading.
We're the devils of the ocean,
We're the fearsome, killing, robbing pirates of the deep
Who destroy white horses galloping across the shore.

Jack Tregunna (10)
Bishop Henderson CE Primary School, Taunton

Treehouse Territory

In our treehouse territory,
Our lives are just fine,
In our treehouse territory,
We're always on cloud nine.

In our treehouse kingdom,
Birds sing from heaven,
In our treehouse kingdom,
Happiness is 24/7.

In our treehouse realm,
We have a bird's eye view of the city.
In our treehouse realm,
It really is quite pretty.

In our treehouse territory,
Our lives are just fine,
In our treehouse territory,
We're always on cloud nine.

Tomass Penny (10)
Bishop Henderson CE Primary School, Taunton

Friends Land

F riends forever, that's what friendship is about.
R unning and playing swings and roundabouts.
I t's kindness and caring, it's laughing and sharing.
E ndless hours of Lego whatever the weather.
N ew friends, old friends, are all friends together.
D oing whatever friends love and that's being altogether.
S leepovers are made on Saturdays and that's a world of friendship.

Tessa Burge (8)
Bishop Henderson CE Primary School, Taunton

Farm City

In Farm City,
Everything's witty,
I'm the farmer,
Trying to make it calmer.
In the field with the pigs,
Chickens are wearing wigs,
In the tree sits a sheep,
While the chicken drives a jeep.
Meanwhile the parrot plays with the cow
And a horse brushes his bushy eyebrow,
Come and visit us in Farm City
And bring along your bright red kitty.

Ethan Shuttleworth (8)
Bishop Henderson CE Primary School, Taunton

Food World

In this world of food
Everything tastes so good
There are so many lovely treats
Some of them are so hard to beat.

The grass is cheesy
And the trees are breezy
There is chocolate mud
You will always land with a thud.

The time has come
It's where we come from
For in this world of food
Everything tastes so good.

Lilianne Mariyam Liju (11)
Bishop Henderson CE Primary School, Taunton

Yum Yum Land

Minecraft, Minecraft, zombies shooting bubblegum.
Candy dogs and candy cats jump and swim as you play with them.
Chocolate fountain lollipops for lamp posts,
Waffles for skyscrapers, candy canes for walking sticks, Tic Tacs for cars,
Bread for hills, trees made of broccoli,
I would like to be there because I could stuff my face.

Lydia Lambert (8)
Bishop Henderson CE Primary School, Taunton

Christmas World

Every day is Christmas in my world.
I hear happy kids with presents and laughing.
I see chilly snowmen guarding gardens.
I smell warm, sugary, cinnamon scent.
I taste delicious peppermint candy canes.
I touch frosty trees and cold snow.
I love Christmas.

Brayden Carl John Fitzgerald (8)
Bishop Henderson CE Primary School, Taunton

Puppy

P uppies
U p and far away, the puppies come to play
P omeranians prance and pounce
P apillons eat parsnips
Y et poodles eat noodles.

Esther Lambert (8)
Bishop Henderson CE Primary School, Taunton

The Revenge Of The Kreepers

Nightmare, nightmare,
Scare, scare, scare,
If you want to stop it, eat a pear.
Creepy-crawlies come out at night,
They suck your blood and say goodnight.

Alexander James Coles (8)
Bishop Henderson CE Primary School, Taunton

Beautiful Snow Land

Beautiful Snow Land glittering with snow,
So beautiful with the extreme perfect glow.
Fairy tales are told, as the day goes on,
In the beautiful land we all shine out.
We sing along all together on the glistening ice.
Friends come together to play on the snow and ice,
While the villagers talk along.
Beautiful Snow Land here I come,
To meet my friends and play along.
All together we sing, all together we dance,
All together we roam,
I'm never leaving this land,
Beautiful home, my place where I live.
Land that is so adorable, you won't
want to leave it.
Beautiful world, I hope I find another one like the
one I live in.

Lachezar Petrov Genchev (9)
Carrant Brook Junior School, Northway

The Land Of Endless Fun

Chocolate and sweets
Lots of treats
Yum, yum, yum
In the land of endless fun.

Bouncy castles
All no hassle
Don't forget snowball fights
But they're white.

Tyrannosaurus rexes are pink
Which makes the hippos wink
Everyone runs and always win
And the fishes all have fins.

But some days the land of endless fun is boring
So the folks in it just lie around the
castle while snoring.

Lilly-Mae Lawrence (8)
Carrant Brook Junior School, Northway

Scream City's Theme Park

In this city,
No one's pretty,
This makes you shiver,
Like a clown eating your liver.

Whatever you see,
Will not let you be,
Hide in a tree,
Then you'll be free.

When you see a zombie crawl,
It must be hungry if you see it drool,
This is not your dream,
Even if it seems.

If you see the river flow,
It sounds like a creeper about to blow.

Jaiden Maggs (10)
Carrant Brook Junior School, Northway

In The Twisted Woods

In the twisted woods,
Everyone wears hoods.
The trees are black and scary,
Though their leaves are hairy.

There is just one house,
Inhabited by a mouse.
The mouse is very tall,
He will make you seem small.

If you think this place is fun,
Be careful or you may run.
Make sure you prepare,
For you may get a scare.

Niall Baker (11)
Carrant Brook Junior School, Northway

Nightmare Night

Spooky noises keep you up at night,
Maybe they just want a fight.

Getting out bed,
Seeing blood that is red.

Exploring spooky places,
When you could be at some races.

The mazes will be hard,
Because you are crouching like lard.

There are so many doors,
Which way to go to an applause.

Drew Baker (9)
Carrant Brook Junior School, Northway

Digging For Gold

Once I was digging for gold,
My brother told me, "Don't go down to the mines
Or you'll be killed easily."
Then I found a village of souls, who set me free;
So I could be me and live happily;
With my family, in peace and tranquillity.

Ben Nicholls (8)
Carrant Brook Junior School, Northway

Candy Land

C an you think of all the sweets you can have?
A world is made of candy that is where all the sweets are
N o one doesn't like sweets
D o you like Mars bars and Twix?
Y ou can have all the sweets if you go there!

Emily Goodchild (8)
Carrant Brook Junior School, Northway

Minecraft Pocket Edition

I like Minecraft.
Sports in Minecraft are football, basketball and more.
In Minecraft I like music.
I like magic and mods.
I play Minecraft on my PlayStation.

Zhaniyan Nikolov (10)
Carrant Brook Junior School, Northway

The Land Of The Wild

The land of the wild is a dangerous place,
A frightening place, a monstrous place,
The land of the wild of full of beasts,
Big and small and fierce.

Great monsters roam there, or so I've heard,
Some have wings like a bird!
Full of life, the forests are,
Never quiet, never far.

The land of the wild is a dangerous place,
A frightening place, a monstrous place.
The land of the wild is a crazy place,
That's why I'll never go!

Mimi Colman-Deveney (11)
Combe Down CE Primary School, Combe Down

Music Land

In music land everyone is mad
The melody is very sad
Everyone has a song to sing
Even the mice squeak and ding.

We make noise
When the horses doze
Once we have a song
We ding dong!

Tristan Graham (9)
Exford CE First School, Exford

Volcano Land Acrostic

V omiting volcano
O range lava
L ook at the levelling lava
C an't stop it
A ngry, bursting volcano
N oisy crashes
O nce erupted, always erupting.

Liam Callaert (8)
Exford CE First School, Exford

Horse Land Sense Poem

I hear happy horses neighing in the field,
I see the hoof marks trampled in the ground,
They taste the Mollichaff.
I smell sweet hay coming from the feeders,
I touch the warm fur of my horses.

Emily Violet Illing (8)
Exford CE First School, Exford

Nightmare World

I hear the screams
I see a scary pumpkin head
I smell the old food in the fridge
I taste fear
I touch an old phone
Terrifying nightmares.

Charlie Colin Glover (8)
Exford CE First School, Exford

Candy

Candy, candy is very sweet,
It's not like potatoes and it's not like meat.
My favourite candy is strawberry laces,
I eat them in lots of different places.
My mummy gives me lots of treats,
Sometimes I hide under my sheets.

Erin Summer Kay (7)
Greatfield Park Primary School, Up Hatherley

Dinosaur Fun

D reams come true
I magination runs wild
N o wild dinosaurs
O MG, best place ever
S uperb.

George Stone (7)
Greatfield Park Primary School, Up Hatherley

Candy Park

C ats miaowing noisily
A s the sun gleams bright
N ow the animals are awake
D oing their middle day walks as they always do
Y ou do what you want, I don't mind

W ow, it's such an amazing sight
O h, it's so much fun
R ight now, why don't you come on down
L et's hang out, nothing boring because there's just fun, fun, fun
D o and eat as much as you like.

Libby Boobyer (10)
Hamp Academy, Bridgwater

Hero Island

H eroes zoom across the sky
E very moment is power
R ight now everyone is having fun
O h no, villains are attacking

"I will save you," say the heroes
S uper quick, the heroes save everyone
L uckily, everyone is okay
A nd no one is hurt
N o one is ever safe
D o you have superpowers?

Lewis Watts (10)
Hamp Academy, Bridgwater

Halloween World

Every day is Halloween in my world,
Where the trees are dark and gloomy
And the shadows come out to play.
The witches use their black magic,
To cast their wicked spells
And the bony skeletons like to jiggle.
The big Frankenstein likes to stomp around the haunted house.
I love Halloween world.

Mia Parker
Hamp Academy, Bridgwater

My World

My world is tasty,
But the trees are a bit pasty.
The bread is a little toasty,
That's because people are boasty.
In my wonderful city,
Everything's pretty!
My heart is pounding
And all the lions are rounding.
It's now time for me to go,
I will see you at home.

Skye Godbeer
Hamp Academy, Bridgwater

All About The Unicorn

U nicorns are magical
N ot everyone believes in unicorns
I f you don't believe, who are you?
C an you find one?
O ff in a fantasy land they lie
R unning off in the sunset
N ow go off and find one
S ome will say they're fake.

Connie Sara Valerie Downton (8)
Hamp Academy, Bridgwater

Magic Land

M agic there is all around her
A nd there is a mermaid
G enies are in this place and unicorns
I would like to live there
C an you imagine living there? It would be cool!

Sophia Alcantara (9)
Hamp Academy, Bridgwater

Cloud City

Up in Cloud City where the clouds are always fluffy
With cloud bunnies
Where water comes down from the sky
And that's where butterflies fly
Now you know what Cloud City looks like.

Ava Daniells (9)
Hamp Academy, Bridgwater

Chocolate Rainbow Land

Shimmering, glimmering,
Sparkling sun, rainbows rising and whispering,
Tall trees,
Gliding unicorns, fairies, dinosaurs,
I love them all.
Yes, I love them all.

Isobel Ferguson (9)
Hamp Academy, Bridgwater

Tasty Town

Amongst the soft, pink candyfloss trees,
Where the rainbow gummy bears live,
Lies the gummiest town of all.
Tasty Town!
There's a gingerbread house
And a chocolate waterfall.
Not forgetting the fizzy UFOs,
As well as the sugar snow,
In Tasty Town you can't resist gobbling it up!

Evie John (8)
Haselbury Plucknett First School, Haselbury Plucknett

Soldiers

S oldiers going
O ver and away
L et's work together while we pray
D efinitely we will be sad
I s it you? I see you there
E very twist has its turn
R ather have you here every day.

Daisy-Mae Suzie Valentine (9)
Hugh Sexey CE Middle School, Blackford

The Colossal World Far Up High

There's a colossal world far up high,
To get there you need to fly.
Once you reach it in the sky,
You'll have to avoid little gnomes that lie.

In the buildings perched on clouds,
Little gnomes live in shrouds.
They're always trying to protect their grounds,
They have a currency other than pounds.

Years ago, in 1891,
People got sent in a rocket labelled 1,
But because of the loss of gravity up there,
The people got stuck in the air.

Now the people have become the gnomes
And are very protective of their homes,
If anyone comes and lands in front of their toes.

Janis Lusitis (11)
Huish Episcopi Primary School, Huish Episcopi

The Land Of Candy

In the land of candy,
Everything's handy,
There might be a treat
For you all to eat.

There are candy cane trees
And yellow, gummy bees,
There's a special sherbet flower,
That unicorns all devour.

Chocolate exploding cupcakes
And sprinkles left over from earthquakes,
Sugar that looks like snow
And lollipops that make you glow.

Pixies eating ice cream
And little chocolate mice scream,
Houses made of gingerbread
And little children getting fed.

Thank you everyone for taking your time
And listening to my little rhyme.

Lola James (10)
Huish Episcopi Primary School, Huish Episcopi

The Land Of Dinosaurs

D iplodocus is the tallest dinosaur that feeds on leaves
I n Dino Land, the dinos hunt around for their food
N ow the garudimimus is the fastest one speeding around
O pen sea is where the pterodactyls find their fish
S tegosauruses have spikes all over their backs like a thin book
A nkylosaurus has like a boulder on the end of its tail
U nder the sea is a walrus but a walrus that can eat a shark in one go
R unning around the trees is a raptor
S till speeding around is the garudimimus.

Euan Robertson (10)
Huish Episcopi Primary School, Huish Episcopi

The Land Of Lost Beasts

Terrifying, terrifying, terrifying,
Fire and embers flooded everywhere,
Mystery, nightmares and fear work and scare,
Cerberus and Hydra tear bones to bits,
Whilst the sphinx waits to tell his riddle,
To those who are silly enough to end up there.
The skeletons catch a sight of life and snatch you,
Then throw you into an abyss of blackness.
You fall and fall, then land before the lord
of the underworld.
"You're dead!" is what he yelled at me.
I barely heard this before my spirit really and
truly died.

Emma-Jane Keegan (10)
Huish Episcopi Primary School, Huish Episcopi

The Between Universe

A land where legends run free
The way it's meant to be
Unicorns are deranged
Dragons' fire is short-ranged

Unicorns are as wild as can be
Dragons are proud, gentle and free
Powerful Hydra as weak as a feather
Valuable Pegasus now with skin like leather

Graceful phoenix clumsy as can be
Wild griffins bound, never to be free
Now you see we are reverse
This place between you and the parallel universe

But this is our home
In our world shaped like a dome.

Matilda Valerie Stuckey (10)
Huish Episcopi Primary School, Huish Episcopi

Candy Village

C hocolate ice cream covers the fields,
A pples drowned in toffee,
N ougat acts as pillows to sleep on,
D elicious cupcakes tasty and sweet,
Y ou need to come to my village to have a feast.

V illagers are so sweet,
I love the candy, it's so yummy,
L ittle gummy worms in the ground,
L ollies grow like a plant,
A mazing gingerbread on the lane,
G ummies are a big treat,
E verything in my village you can eat.

Kyla Baker (10)
Huish Episcopi Primary School, Huish Episcopi

Cheese Land

C razy Cheese Land is
H ectic, the people are
E ating all the time, day and night, they
E at everything in sight they do
S lithery cheese snakes eat up mice, they must
E at as much as possible while it's still there

L unatic the king is
A nd stop we must
N aughty the people are
D airylea is the richest, it is.

(Read in Yoda voice.)

Ellis Beake (10)
Huish Episcopi Primary School, Huish Episcopi

The Lyrical Land Of Books

In the land of brilliant books,
You may take lots of looks,
You may take a peer
And no one shall sneer.

There are lots of pages,
Read books about mages,
The mischievous mice eat books,
While the townsfolk give them dirty looks!

Find books in nooks (and crannies),
Books about sweet, old grannies,
You can have lots of fun
And when you are done,
Take a look in one of our books!

Magnus Haines (10)
Huish Episcopi Primary School, Huish Episcopi

The Land Of The Dinosaurs

In the land of the dinosaurs,
Somewhere far away,
On a distant star,
Not a person in sight,
Where is this place?

There isn't a thing in sight,
Dry as the desert,
There's a volcanic volcano here,
The sauropods stride over there.

Nothing is alive here,
But the ridiculous reptiles hear,
Don't come here,
You know you shouldn't,
Just turn around and flee.

Uday Akshay Patel (9)
Huish Episcopi Primary School, Huish Episcopi

By Cupcake Mountain

Hey, hey, hey, come and play,
Scoff, nibble and stuff,
Eat everything in sight,
Mountains of cupcakes and trees are broccoli,
(I don't think anyone will eat them!)
Streams of yummy, fun, melted candy
And lettuce leaves for grass.
Oh no, it's raining, but that's okay,
Because it rains gummy bears
And all sorts of chocolate.
When it snows you get white chocolate mice.

Hatty (11)
Huish Episcopi Primary School, Huish Episcopi

The Land Of No Return

There is a place
Where skeletons cackle
And the floor is made of bones.

There is a place
That sleeps underground
With rotting trees and dying flowers.

There is a place
That is bloated with evil
And where shadowy creatures roam the land.

But there is also a place
Where the sky is blue and the clouds are white
And the ground is full of flowers.

Kaia-Lara Hammond (11)
Huish Episcopi Primary School, Huish Episcopi

Gummy Land

In Gummy Land,
Everything's grand,
Everyone likes it all,
Even the chocolate pool.

There isn't any meat,
But the food will touch your feet
And where you get the sweets,
You'll get the treats.

It is here where you can stuff your face,
In this amazing place,
Where we have a gummy mountain,
We also have a chocolate fountain.

Alfie Cook (10)
Huish Episcopi Primary School, Huish Episcopi

Dream Island

My world is a dream land,
Where you could be a star in a band,
Or a unicorn,
Just being born.

A dream of yours is here,
Candy canes are near,
Dragons are free, spitting out fire
And you will be full of fear.

Choose your dream,
It could be ice cream
And will come true,
It could howl or make a boo!
Your dream will come true.

Emily Anne Wheller (10)
Huish Episcopi Primary School, Huish Episcopi

Land Of Food

In the land of food,
There is a salad pool,
With veg galore,
There's nothing more you could wish for.

Near the sea,
There is algae,
But it is made of peas.

You stay in a house,
Where you will not find a mouse,
The carpets are swede
And the armchairs are peas.

Come to this place,
Where you can stuff your face.

Bella (10)
Huish Episcopi Primary School, Huish Episcopi

Nightmare World

If you are brave
And not scared of a cave,
Then come here,
Where it's all fear.

There are broccoli trees
And loads of peas,
There is a big, scary clown,
That always wears a frown.
There is a big, furry spider,
Who killed a childminder.

It's all dark,
Sometimes you may hear a dog bark.

Jasmine (9)
Huish Episcopi Primary School, Huish Episcopi

My Pet Dinosaur

On a tropical island in the middle of the sea,
Stood a vast dinosaur right next to me,
No matter how much he would try,
He could just not eat a fish pie.

He is a T-rex,
His name is Trex,
He starred in Jurassic Park,
He even sailed on the Jurassic ark.

My pet dinosaur is awesome!

Luke Padfield (10)
Huish Episcopi Primary School, Huish Episcopi

The Land Of Dreams

D are to dream, dream to dare
R esolutions hang in the air
E xaggerate don't you dare, dreams are happy don't you know?
A stonishing stuff you can achieve, don't give up if you believe
M agnificent magic in the jars, a fairy tale that can be ours.

Samuel Lyes (11)
Huish Episcopi Primary School, Huish Episcopi

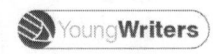

Fairy Tale Town

Fairies fly high in the sky,
Whilst knights on stallions go riding by.
A glass slipper on the palace stairs,
A tower full of Rapunzel's hairs.
Oh look, Humpty Dumpty and Jack Horner,
But danger is round every corner.
Seven different dwarves living in a house,
One angry, another as shy as a mouse.
Three houses made from straw, brick and twig,
Followed by a wolf that's bad and big.
Pricked on the finger by a spinning wheel,
A princess who an evil fairy wanted to kill.
A little girl who stole some porridge,
Some goats who tried to cross a bridge,
To wake them they need a kiss, pure and true,
A beanstalk so high you could see if you flew,
A girl in a red cape and a brown bear,
There are stories everywhere.

Livia Brain (10)
Moorlands Junior School, Bath

Cloud Cuckooland

C loud Cuckooland
L iquorice portal door
O range, lime, strawberry and more
U nicorn as calm as can be
D ark chocolate waterfall lands on me

C haotic people always flappy
U nicorns, pink, orange and happy
C hocolate, glistening, warm pond
K ittens and unicorns have a special bond
O utrageous hospital always late
O utstanding house can even inflate!
L ego sleepyhead wakes when you shout, "Boom!"
A nd a pet dog's guarding the meeting room
N o bad guys allowed in this land
D o you agree or will you be banned?

Abby Elizabeth Susan Hunter (8)
North Nibley CE Primary School, North Nibley

Marshmallow Mansion

If you dig and dig beneath the ocean,
Eventually you'll find a potion,
If you drink this bottle straight,
You may feel the world vibrate.
Slowly falling faster and faster,
You may feel a wall of plaster,
Then at the bottom you land with a bump,
In a marshmallow tree by a marshmallow stump,
A sweet-smelling smell of a marshmallow cake,
But the bakers are not all wide awake,
All was well till I came into sight,
The marshmallow people hit me with all their might,
I stumbled and staggered through the marshmallow street,
It sounds very nice bit it's really not a treat,
On and on through the mystical land,
After a while you'll find a band,
Straight away put that band on
And in a few seconds you will be gone,
Up and through this old, broken root,
There are marshmallow kittens all very cute,

You'll find a beautiful china bowl
And in this bowl you will find a scroll.
If you open this scroll, you see a tantrum
And at the top it will say, 'Marshmallow Mansion'!

Joss Reynard (9)
North Nibley CE Primary School, North Nibley

Catopia

What if the first cat in space found a planet,
A safe place for cats to inhabit?
It's called Catopia, it's up in the air,
It's guaranteed to make a human stare.
For those stupid humans it looks like a dump,
For those clever cats it looks like a beautiful lump.
To get into this planet you need a cat paw print,
Guess what's in there? I'll give you a hint
And if you get into this planet of cats,
Don't bother to look at your unhelpful maps.
For if you walk just south of the woods,
I'll tell you once you really should
Do what I tell you, you'll find a house,
Not big enough for humans, not small enough for a mouse.
In that house you find a kitten,
That kitten will go by the name of Mitten.
If you take her under your wing,
You'll find her useful on your journey in.
Then you'll reach the scratching post mansion,
Say to the queen, "I'm not here to tantrum,

I come in peace, please let me stay,
It's my dream to be a cat someday!"

Delphie Locke (9)
North Nibley CE Primary School, North Nibley

Macaca World

Welcome to Macaca World,
Mr Cheesestring's here to see you,
He's one of a kind, a very great guy
And always wears bright blue.

By the candy tree,
You're sure to see,
Mr Lollipop sat on a rock,
With a broken knee
And a cup of tea,
Wait till you see him pop!

The sun is always shining,
It is smiling,
Mr Lollipop's gingerbread house is amazing,
People stare at it gazing.
Mr Sweet is a mouse,
He really does have an underground house.

The Macaca café is a great place,
The waiter has a cupcake face!
The sweet, sugary grass,
Doesn't taste like glass.

Amelie Ivy de Pass (8)
North Nibley CE Primary School, North Nibley

Unicorn Universe

In the town there is a happy rainbow,
It sings a lullaby every night,
She changes its pink colour from dark to light,
The rainbow shares love with a happy delight.
In the town there are happy, fun stairs,
They love to eat cupcakes.
When you go up the stairs, off it takes,
But when you go down them they feel like lakes.
The streams smell like strawberries,
The sun makes it sparkly, the moon
makes it bright,
And it's beautiful and nice.
The houses are sweet,
Unicorns spread magic all around the houses.
This place is so good, you should be there,
You really should.

Beea Ward (7)
North Nibley CE Primary School, North Nibley

Gingerbread Street

Gingerbread Street is very sweet,
Its houses are made of ginger,
With multicoloured Smarties as tiles on roofs
And icing to keep it together,
Little gingerbread people live inside,
With eyes as green as grass,
Smell the sweet smell,
As icing cars go zooming past, whisking you
off the floor,
See the fields full of crops,
They glisten in the sun,
It makes you want to taste,
The taste of gingery fun,
The hedges are made of ginger,
Dyed with green food colouring,
Try not to eat them, although they seem yummy,
Gingerbread Street is full of things to eat!

Emily Rea (8)
North Nibley CE Primary School, North Nibley

Chocolate City

Welcome to Chocolate City,
The creamy chocolate waterfall never ends,
If you drink the chocolate water,
You might have a tasty treat.
The shops always look good enough to eat,
The chocolate hotel never runs out of rooms.
If you go near the funfair, you may
hear big booms,
That's because of the rides and slides.
The houses will always be free,
The chocolate woods tempt you to eat
a chocolate tree.
You will never run out of chocolate rings,
There are lots of absolutely amazing things,
So don't be shy,
Now I will say goodbye.

Nathan George Hunter (8)
North Nibley CE Primary School, North Nibley

Zombie Village

Z ombie Village is cruel and rotten
O ut in the wild you can see
M ore zombies than you could ever see
B eware!
I n case an army comes after you
E ven if there's one it will be quite hard to handle

V ery victorious village
I s under attack
L isten to the zombies before they go back
L ook across
A nd see the pitch-black mansion
G hosts wander down the black corridor
E ternally scaring anyone who dares to enter.

Ollie Perry (8)
North Nibley CE Primary School, North Nibley

Candy Cloud

C ute, cuddly candyfloss bunnies hop,
A nd you can have as many sweets as you like,
N o people who are mean are allowed in.
D o you like a sweet? Then this place will be a treat.
Y ummy river of chocolate milkshake. Come on in and take.

C ome to a place where you can stuff your face.
L ucky people only go here.
O n your birthday you will get a giant lollipop.
U mbrellas are made of sherbet.
D o you know this world is a treat?

Olivia Prosser (8)
North Nibley CE Primary School, North Nibley

Candy, Candy, Candy

C andy is the best, candy, candy, candy
A ndy the candy minister
N o to no candy
D o eat, eat and eat
Y ummy candy

C andy everywhere
A block of flats in a cup of cola
N o to no sweets
D o have parties
Y ummy car

C andy and candy
A ndy eats cakes in his gummy house
N o to no cake
D o gobble everything
Y ummy time.

Jude James l'Anson (8)
North Nibley CE Primary School, North Nibley

Candy Villa

C andy Village is the best.
A ndy the candy makes the rest.
N ever say no to delicious candy.
D efinitely say yes to the candy seller, Mandy!
Y ou will like it if you try.

V ery much you will buy.
I will love it forever and so will you.
L ollipop forest is scary. Boo!
L ive forever and so will I.
A life in Candy Villa you must try.

Oliver Pitt (8)
North Nibley CE Primary School, North Nibley

Candy Cane Cave

Flying high in the beautiful sky, you'll never believe,
The things you spy, or what you could achieve.

Come down to the magical ground,
There are lots of special things to do.
Chloe the cupcake fairy is waiting just for you!

Clouds are as hard as candy sticks,
Houses are made of candy cane bricks.

Candy Cane castle high in the sky,
If you want to get there, you need to fly.

Hannah Jade Stanulewicz (8)
North Nibley CE Primary School, North Nibley

Candy Cave

Candy Cave is the most wonderful planet
in the galaxy.
Candy canes for a crossing.
The top of the trees are as fluffy as candyfloss.
When we say rain, it rains Skittles,
But it can be quite annoying.
All of the houses are covered in candy,
The flowers are as dazzling as disco lights.
The unicorns have lollies for horns.
All of the stars are made of biscuits,
Whatever you can imagine.

Cara Sophia Saunderson (8)
North Nibley CE Primary School, North Nibley

About In Game Land

In a magical land called Game Land
Is a giant Stampy statue
He is worshipped by the people, the gamers and the characters
Tastes like pineapple, sea and dog
Smells like Xbox, lollies and logs
The ore floor has every YouTuber's name in a star
The boss of Game Land is the admin
But his proper name is Romeo
In the sky the sun stops, slowly as video games pass by.

Elliot Pretlove (7)
North Nibley CE Primary School, North Nibley

Candy City

C andy City is the best
A nd you have the time to rest
N ever forget what you met
D o you regret?
Y ou can eat whatever!

C an you have a river of flavour?
I t rains chewy bubblegum and melting candyfloss
T ry the stairs that are made of marshmallows
Y ou'd better remember this place or...

Ella Rose Thomson (9)
North Nibley CE Primary School, North Nibley

Unicorn Village

Unicorns playing all around
They run and play along candyfloss ground
Rainbows racing as they fly
Rainbow flowers rising up to the sky
Pink pebbles perching on the pot
The sky is the most beautiful of the lot
The grass is as green as a tree
Snow is as salty as can be
These are the things that may seem
Like they are from a unicorn's dream.

Grace Hall (7)
North Nibley CE Primary School, North Nibley

Teddy Town!

In Teddy Town you can see Ra-Ra the Teddy Boss opening the sky castle.
You can hear the sound of metal slicing robots.
You can touch the special statue and the portal.
You can eat the fence of candy,
Mandy owns the goat gate,
The castle is grand.
Stampy will meet you by the gate
And you can see the ten robot rumble in the corner of Teddy Town.

George Loveday (7)
North Nibley CE Primary School, North Nibley

Block To Block

I live in Blocky Block,
I work at musical mine,
When I mine the blocks,
They mimic all the time.

One day my boss said to me,
"Build a wall to protect us."
So I travelled in my blue boat,
On the rough seas.

When I was there,
Lava was smothered,
All tidy and neat,
So I poured water that was salted.

Seb Bouvier (9)
North Nibley CE Primary School, North Nibley

Unicorn World

Welcome to Unicorn World,
It is full of magic,
Unicorn World is powerful,
Unicorn World is wonderful,
Unicorn World is full of very nice unicorns.
Sparkle is in charge of it, she is very fantastic,
It never rains in Unicorn World,
No, not at all,
No, nothing happens in Unicorn World,
Yes, that is right.

Isabella Spiller (8)
North Nibley CE Primary School, North Nibley

Reaper Road

On Reaper Road, the reaper is quick,
Some people say he's as fast as Saint Nick.
Enter his house if you dare,
If you go in, you'll get a great scare!
It's Reaper rock you need,
This rock will save your life and soul
And make sure you won't bleed.

Jacob Mydlowski (7)
North Nibley CE Primary School, North Nibley

Wizard Wonderland

In Wizard Wonderland, wizards galore,
Merlin is the chief, he doesn't have a sword.
Excalibur in the stone, shining in the light,
Vampires on the hill, howling horrible sounds,
Crying for blood and rotten flesh.

Zak Lampard (8)
North Nibley CE Primary School, North Nibley

Haunted Street

I hear the crunch of bones,
I see purple sky as it changes to grey,
I smell guts and livers turning rotten,
I taste chunky chicken wings,
I touch jumping brains and pumping hearts.

I love Halloween!

Freddy Romero-Brown (9)
North Nibley CE Primary School, North Nibley

Adventure In A Daydream

Halloween world is scary,
I can see a zombie eating a fairy.
Ghosts are flying in mid-air,
Skeletons retreat back into their lair.
It's not very pleasant here,
I wonder if there is another world near.
I can see a helping hand in the sky,
So to Halloween I say goodbye.
The land of my ancestors I'm now in,
Time to explore my forgotten kin.
Kings and queens with knights in battle,
I am now sowing crops and herding cattle,
Dodging disease like plague and pox and scurvy,
To Belfast next to make Titanic seaworthy.
I go through a door and join a special day,
The VE Day celebrations are underway.
I suddenly hear my teacher's voice,
Sadly, I have no choice.
I open my eyes without delay,
"Finish your work then go out to play."

Theia-Rose Williams (10)
Parkend Primary School, Parkend

Unicorn Unicorn

Unicorn, unicorn, in the sky
Unicorn, unicorn, fly so high
My land is pink, purple and fluffy too
All I can hear is 'I love you'
Unicorn, unicorn, with your horn so bright
Flashing like Skittles all through the night
Unicorn, unicorn, gone in a dash
Unicorn, unicorn, flash, flash, flash
Unicorn, unicorn, as fluffy as can be
Unicorn, unicorn, always flies free.

Do you believe in unicorns?
I do!

Sonni Powell (7)
Parkend Primary School, Parkend

Superhero, Superhero

My land is Superhero Land
Where there's no sand
Just wood which makes it good.

My superhero is mighty and brave
He always wants to help and save
As a villain comes along
He sings his superhero song.

He stands up tall
Waiting for a call
And when it comes he's on his way
With no pay!

My superhero is mighty and brave
He always wants to help and save!

Brayden Powell (7)
Parkend Primary School, Parkend

Do Dreams Come True?

Dreams do come true!
It might happen to you.
Make a wish,
Swirl and swish,
Dream of things you love.

The tunnel of your mind,
Dogs are barking but kind,
Candy cane hills
And sherbet mills,
Are some of the things to love.

There's raspberry ice,
That tastes nice,
Spinning sweets in the air,
Just like a funfair,
You can go there in your dreams!

Seth Waller (6)
Parkend Primary School, Parkend

The Forest At Night

The forest at night.
It's like nowhere that you've ever been
And like nothing that you've seen.
Creatures come out from their dens,
The forest is where the fun never ends.
The forest at night.

Ella Jones (10)
Parkend Primary School, Parkend

Classic Dinosaur

C laws are very sharp.
L ong ago there was a big dino.
A mazing, cool dinosaur.
S harp claws, razor teeth,
S melly poo,
I gnorant, smelly dinosaur,
C lassic dude.

D ancing dino,
I rresistable,
N obbly knees,
O ne of a kind,
S cary dude,
A nnoying sucker,
U tterly annoying,
R unning dude.

Rhys Friend (8)
St Mary's CE Primary School, Writhlington

Snow Land

S now is very cool
N ow I can make a snowman
O utside there's ice everywhere
W ind and snow are amazing

L ands are pretty
A nd I can go on my sledge
N ow make a snow angel
D aniel is very happy.

David Shave (7)
St Mary's CE Primary School, Writhlington

Rainbow Land

In Rainbow Land, everything is rainbow.
There is a rainbow stream with underwater music,
With rainbow animals, sweet like candy.
There are rainbow houses.
Not a speck of wood in Rainbow Land.
There's magic in every step you take.

Hollie Davies (8)
St Mary's CE Primary School, Writhlington

Sweetie

S weet Land
W here you can eat sweets
E very day and
E very night
T ill you go home
I magine
E ating sweets all day.

Shylah (7)
St Mary's CE Primary School, Writhlington

Candy Land

C ity full of candy, it's so sweet and tasty
A nd it is so, so sweet, you'll love to stay here for weeks. Chocolate bunnies are your pets.
N ear the chocolate fountain there are ginger houses.
D are to go in the Creme Egg bed and taste them.
Y ou like candy, stay here for months, ice cream clouds, it rains Vimto.

L ove the Slush Puppies with people swimming
A nd gummy bear babies, they are jelly beans.
N ap all you want, your blanket is strawberry,
D ream of sweets, dinner made for you.

Ellie Sanderson (8)
St Michael's CE First School, Minehead

Sport Is The Best

S wimming in the sea
P ool is a type of place you swim in
O ccasionally you get a lot of money if you play sport
R emember your equipment you need for your sport
T ennis is a type of sport, sport is healthy for you

I like sport
S port is good

T he best sport is football
H ealthiness you get from sport
E very sport is good

B e the king of sport
E veryone should do it
S port is epic
T here are a lot of them.

Dylan Dean Newby (8)
St Michael's CE First School, Minehead

Underwater Land

U nderwater you'll hear the sound of the dolphins singing
N othing better than blue bubblegum
D own on the golden sand you'll find lots of pearls
E verything feels like a dream!
R ed coral leaves swaying side to side
W hales blowing water out of their spouts
A miracle mermaid, as pretty as a rainbow
T he underwater world has lots of sea creatures
E xcited to swim under the deep blue sea
R ain falling to make the sea higher.

Grace Hughes (8)
St Michael's CE First School, Minehead

I Feel Like I'm Living In A Dream

I feel like I'm living in a dream,
Where the clouds are made of ice cream.
Flying in a rocket through the sky
And wave as we whizz by.
I feel like I'm free when I'm living in a dream
And I'm walking around in my blue, blue jeans.
I'm right here, right now, you can't take it from me,
Because it's my world, my life, my lovely dream.
So go away and leave me be
And if you want to come and join me,
All you've got to do is believe.

Sonny Newman (9)
St Michael's CE First School, Minehead

Water World

U nderwater World
N ever-ending land
D evils are not allowed in my world
E ffective, golden creatures live on the fragile floor
R are species of crabs and fish hibernate here
W ater World is blue, large, dangerous and never-ending
A large, beautiful, brittle flooring
T iger sharks, goblin sharks and great white sharks here
E ating things creep across the delicate flooring
R emarkable things happen.

Luca Gasperini (7)
St Michael's CE First School, Minehead

Ghosts Are A Nightmare

Ghosts coming through your door, creeping in the night,
Looking out for you, keeping out of sight.
They start walking step by step, not making a sound,
But then on a small pillow they see something small, yellow and round.
It's the child, he awakes and screams with power,
But now it's time for the ghosts to go back to their ghost tower.
Bye-bye ghosts, we will see you again, maybe tomorrow, maybe next week, maybe another day.

Jade Clark (8)
St Michael's CE First School, Minehead

Sugary Sweet Land

Candy, candy, the best land ever!
I love candy!

Candy is scrummy and delicious,
In sugary Sweet Land.

There's gingerbread
And sugary, fantastic stuff.

In Candy Land there's a rainbow and chocolate rivers,
By the side of the cake shop made of cake.

There are lollipops and a chocolate fountain,
With magical bunnies and yummy frosting snowmen as well,
With lots of sweets everywhere.

Olivia Katie Glenn (9)
St Michael's CE First School, Minehead

The Spooky Street

I'm walking down my street,
When I hear a loud *beep, beep*.
I retreat to a cave,
But there are dodo birds that eat your brains.
I poke my head out of the cave,
But I see a creepy killer clown
And it is heading straight down town.
Now it's finally day,
I hear a human being eaten as prey.
Come listen now, but when it's night,
You might have a painful fright.

Ollo Rambe (8)
St Michael's CE First School, Minehead

Candy Lands

Crumbs on the floor for candy birds,
All pink and fluffy like candy.
Animals running wild all over the place
for chocolate.
No one has seen the garden,
Gummy bears in the sweet forest.
Do not enter the candy maze,
You will get stuck.
You can hide in the candy,
From the sweet monster,
But he might see you in the candy,
So get away from him.

Charlotte Cottington (8)
St Michael's CE First School, Minehead

Flying Nachos

N achos flying everywhere,
I am scared but still very aware,
G hosts creeping to hide,
H ey everyone, please stay alive!
T he thoughts of being locked up,
M ay scare lots of pups.
A wareness all around,
R esting peace is the only sound.
E veryone is all alarmed,
S ome people harmed.

Eden Coley (9)
St Michael's CE First School, Minehead

Sweets Of Candy!

C andy, candy, in my tummy, because it's good, nice and yummy
A ll is sour, all is plain, everyone loves all sweets the same
N obody hates sweets, because they're just a good, yummy treat
D ouble Decker, super to eat, some as big as you, from your head to your feet
Y ou don't like sweets if it's not your type of treat!

Lucie Matcham (9)
St Michael's CE First School, Minehead

Basketball

B asketball is healthy
A nd very fun.
S erious game but look at all my fans.
K icking not allowed in it.
E verywhere is a basketball pitch.
T all people, small people can play too.
B all is orange and black.
A pple eaters love it.
L ive like one.
L ove basketball forever.

George Dalziel (8)
St Michael's CE First School, Minehead

I Love Dogs!

Animals with four legs are really quite the best,
But there are animals that laugh out loud, like seals, and ones that howl.
I like them all but the one I love best,
Is the one with a cute, little head.
Can you guess?
It's a dog, a cute dog,
Dogs can sniff, dogs can love,
They can sometimes even smell like mud.
I love dogs!

Evie James (8)
St Michael's CE First School, Minehead

Topsy Turvy Underwater Land

In the topsy-turvy underwater land
Everything has a gleam
Like fish in a band
Crabs that scream
While turtles are called Poi
With coral trees
It's full with joy
With rocks shaped like bees
Clams that like to tango
Rays that drink cans
And sharks that eat mango
In the topsy-turvy underwater land.

Chloe Chapman-Humfries (8)
St Michael's CE First School, Minehead

Candy Land!

Candy, candy, in the pot,
Why don't we try and eat the lot!

Candy, candy, we all share,
Gobble, gobble, the pot's now bare.

Candy, candy, red, white, black,
Why don't we open another pack?

Candy, candy, suck, bite, chew,
"Do you want one?"
"Just a few."

Lexi H-A (8)
St Michael's CE First School, Minehead

Basketball

Basketball is good.
Basketball has wood.
Basketball is loud!
Basketballers are proud.
Basketballs are round.
Basketballs are brown.
Basketballers can't kick!
Basketballers are rich!
Basketballers sign.
Basketballers ride.
Basketballers don't drink wine.
Basketballers dine.

Darius Pranciskus Neverauskas (8)
St Michael's CE First School, Minehead

Football

F ootball fans banging
O ffside players in the game
O ff the pitch if you get a red card
T iptoe running in the game
B e the best football player in the team
A quick runner on the field
L is for the losing team
L is for Leeds who always lose.

George Andrew Hall (8)
St Michael's CE First School, Minehead

Candy Land

C andy canes
A ll is yummy
N othing is better
D o you like candy?
Y ummy, gummy candy.

L ovely, gummy surprise
A yummy, gummy prize
N ever give it away, it's too yummy
D id you see the brilliant, excellent, lovely candy?

Ava Butterworth (8)
St Michael's CE First School, Minehead

Candyland

As yummy as a chocolate.
Ice cream as cold as ice.
Candyfloss, as soft as a cloud.
Chocolate rock, as bumpy and lumpy as a twig.
A soft, bouncy, gummy bear as soft
as a trampoline.
Candy cane, as big as a house.
Sugar snow falls.
Sweet and sour yummy dip.
As pretty as a unicorn!

Isla Sapsford (8)
St Michael's CE First School, Minehead

Candy Land

As colourful as a rainbow,
As sweet as dark chocolate crunch,
The land is fluffier than candyfloss!
Sweeter than a berry tree.
As shiny as gold,
Is brighter than the sun,
As soft as multicoloured marshmallow,
As fizzy as cherry coke.
Crazy land of candy!
Come to our sweety shop!

Sophie Hilda Ross (8)
St Michael's CE First School, Minehead

Candy City

C andy is the best
A nd gobstoppers are so sweet
N ow go and eat candy
D o eat gummy strawberries
Y ummy gummy in my tummy

C an you come?
I love candy
T o Candy City
Y ou love candy, don't you?

Christyanna Heath (9)
St Michael's CE First School, Minehead

Friendship

Here at the Friendship it's lovely and warm
I could smell the pies getting baked
I could hear the children laughing
I could feel the happiness
I could see the happy children playing
I could taste the love in the air
I love the Friendship.

Eva Swinburn (8)
St Michael's CE First School, Minehead

Sweet Candy!

C andy, candy is very sour
A nd it's very sweet
N o one likes sweets just plain, but everyone likes them just the same
D rops are sour
Y ou can eat these every day, everyone likes them just the same.

Aiden Fisher (9)
St Michael's CE First School, Minehead

Candy Is The Best

C aramel
A mazing candy
N om nom nom
D ouble Decker
Y ou and me love candy

L ong and sticky
A wesome
N ow let's eat it all
D ummy gummy bears.

Ty Cooper (9)
St Michael's CE First School, Minehead

Animal Land

A nimals are cute
N ewts are not to hug
I n the jungle the lion roars
M aybe I love them all
A nimals are not bad at all
L ions are the kings of the jungle
S nakes are slippy.

Mya Ridehalgh (9)
St Michael's CE First School, Minehead

A Sweet Treat Is Neat

C andy sweets can be a treat
A sweet treat all sugary and neat
N aughty to have, it can rot your teeth
D o you want sugary treats for your supper?
Y ou can have a sweet if it's neat and cool.

Kelsey Clayton (9)
St Michael's CE First School, Minehead

Candyfloss

C andyfloss is as sweet as sugar,
A doughnut as big as the sun,
N ear the chocolate fountain are ginger houses,
D ucks as yellow as the moon,
Y ou like candy trees, you can stay there for weeks.

Sophie-Jo Morton-Watts (7)
St Michael's CE First School, Minehead

Ruler Of Sports

S wimming in the swimming pool
P ool is a type of place that you have fun in
O ccasionally you play football
R emember your sports kit
T ennis is a type of sport
S port is fun to do.

Lenny Mark Morris (8)
St Michael's CE First School, Minehead

Candy Land

C andy Land is the best
A nd the candy cane forest is filled with bears.
N o fruit in the gingerbread houses,
D ays in the lemonade sea.
Y ou should come and see this side of the world.

Maddi Louise Clarke-Jennings (7)
St Michael's CE First School, Minehead

Football

F ans singing songs
O ffside players
O ffside Harry Kane
T o the stadium
B e the best you can!
A ll do your best
L uke in goal
L ike a good goalkeeper.

Luke Brown (7)
St Michael's CE First School, Minehead

Little Nightmares

Little, little nightmares,
Crawling through your head
And stranger things,
Will be created in your head,
With a zombie taking away your good dreams
And spooky, scary skeletons,
Crawling through your mind.

Sid Jack Turner Williams (8)
St Michael's CE First School, Minehead

Football

F ans singing songs,
O ffside balls,
O fficial decision,
T actics,
B attles for the ball,
A mazing skills,
L inesman,
L asting celebrations.

Kaden Michael Owen (8)
St Michael's CE First School, Minehead

Sweet

S weet and sour goofy snacks
W ood coloured chocolate fingers
E clairs full of whipped cream
E very sweet as good as a treat
T arts as nice as candy.

David Bown (7)
St Michael's CE First School, Minehead

The Land Of Dreams

The land of dreams,
Is a place for everyone.
It's where everybody dreams
And if you dream enough,
All the things you dream of,
Come alive in the real world.

Brendan Morley (9)
St Michael's CE First School, Minehead

Candy Land

C andyfloss looking like poodles
A mazing chocolate
N ever leave this place
D elicious, juicy berries
Y um, yum!

Isla May Helena Blustin (7)
St Michael's CE First School, Minehead

Candy Land

Step right into my candy land,
You'll be welcomed in by the Jazzles band.
Candy, candy is everywhere,
If you have a sweet tooth, you'll want to go there.
You'll have so many sweets, you'll want to dance,
Hip, hop, pop, country or trance?
Sugar cane houses and lollipop trees,
Pear drop flowers surrounded by bees,
The gingerbread stars and chocolate cars,
Drive on the roads made of yummy Mars bars.
The grass is strawberry laces,
But the weeds are sour in places.
Watch out, not all is as it seems,
The jelly burst candy shoots squirty beams.
Bouncing here can be handy,
As the clouds are made out of cotton candy.
So if you can bounce and like sweets,
Come here to my land, you'll be in for a treat.

Noah Perkins (7)
Stow On The Wold Primary School, Stow On The Wold

Music Land

M y land is sweet, it's full of treats
U ndo strawberry laces
S kittles for your feet
I gloos have beats
C aramel the band throw treats in the street

L iquorice strings on a bass guitar
A street melody never went so far
N o one wants to leave Music Land
D on't you want to join our band?

Ella White (7)
Stow On The Wold Primary School, Stow On The Wold

Reptile Land

In my world only reptiles live,
In the night, reptiles give you a fright.
Reptiles are the best of the rest,
They are grey and scaly,
They read the paper daily.
So please remember to feed them in November,
Or in the night they will give you a fright.

Alfie Marc Morris (8)
Stow On The Wold Primary School, Stow On The Wold

Candy Land

C andy Land is made out of candy and chocolate
A wesome chocolate skate parks to ride on
N ew candy houses are being built on the streets
D ancing candy canes in the street
Y ou are welcome in Candy Land.

Caleb Austin Willoughby Harvey
Stow On The Wold Primary School, Stow On The Wold

Magic Angels

A bove my head in my bed
N ightly shadows spin around my teds
G rowing and shining as pretty as can be
E legantly
L ovely angels looking after me
S ecretly leaving gifts for free.

Milah Valentine Keyte (7)
Stow On The Wold Primary School, Stow On The Wold

My Forests

Forests are dark,
Forests are made of trees,
Forests can be scary,
Forests have animals in them,
Forests make me want to explore,
Forests need saving,
Forests make me happy!

Darcey Sivalingam
Stow On The Wold Primary School, Stow On The Wold

Kitty

K ittens were miaowing at my feet
I t was amazing
T hey were so fluffy
T his was a once-in-a-lifetime experience
Y es, furballs everywhere!

C ute, cuddly cats
I ncredibly, the houses were made out of fur
T he view was shockingly good
Y ep, it was funny when the laser lamp post turned on.

Peter Ind (10)
Stroud And Cotswold Pupil Referral Services, Stroud

Football World

Mowing the soft, fresh grass,
Ready for the football made from glass.

In this world football fans screaming,
Steven Gerrard scores, people beaming.

Players shouting, "That all is mine!"
Ref yelling, "It's over the line."

Football world is so much fun,
People are happy that their team has won.

Blu Llewellyn (11)
Stroud And Cotswold Pupil Referral Services, Stroud

The Magic Flower

Magic flower, magic flower, where have you been?
You're not there, you're not here,
Please tell me where you seek.
If I was you I'd know, but I am not you so
I do not know,
Unless you're invisible.
But that can't be true.
Do tell me, do tell me, oh please do.
Thank you, oh thank you,
You are true.

Olivia Sophie Mourton (8)
The Richard Pate School, Cheltenham

The Invincible Rabbit

Crunchety! Crunchety! Crunchety! Crunch!
The rabbit has a juicy carrot for lunch
Some rabbits are brown rabbits and some rabbits are black
Crunchety! Crunchety! Crunchety! Crunch!

Hoppety! Hoppety! Hoppety! Hop!
The rabbit is all covered in a top
He walks with a jumpety, jumpety, jumpety, jump
Hippety! Hoppety! Hoppety! Hop!

Crunchety! Crunchety! Crunchety! Crunch!
The rabbit has a juicy carrot for lunch
Some rabbits are brown rabbits and some rabbits are black
Crunchety! Crunchety! Crunchety! Crunch!

Caleb Crook (7)
Wellsprings Primary School, Taunton

The Tiger

Roaridy-roaridy-roaridy-roar,
There goes the tiger with a ferocious jaw.
Some tigers are nice tigers and some
tigers are not,
Roaridy-roaridy-roaridy-roar,
Sounds like it needs some more.

Zigdy-zagdy-zigdy-zag,
There goes the tiger with a shiny, pink bag.
The tiger had a bath and a bit of a laugh,
Zigdy-zagdy-zigdy-zag.

Roaridy-roaridy-roaridy-roar,
There goes the tiger with a ferocious jaw.
Some tigers are nice tigers and some
tigers are not,
Roaridy-roaridy-roaridy-roar.

Theo Crook (7)
Wellsprings Primary School, Taunton

The T-Rex

Chompity-stompity-chompity-stomp,
The dinosaur will eat you with a gulpity big gulp!
Some T-rex are furious and some are not,
Chompity-stompity-chompity-stomp.

Rouchity-ouchity-rouchity-ouch!
The T-rex is coming towards you... ouch!
Some T-rex are scary and some are not,
Rouchity-ouchity-rouchity-ouch!

Chompity-stompity-chompity-stomp,
The dinosaur will eat you with a gulpity big gulp!
Some T-rex are furious and some are not,
Chompity-stompity-chompity-stomp.

Raoul Parnici (8)
Wellsprings Primary School, Taunton

The Parrot

Squawkity-squawkity-squawkity-squawk,
The parrot loves to talk, talk and talk,
Some are colourful and some are not,
Squawkity-squawkity-squawkity-squawk.

Flappity-flappity-flappity-flap,
The parrot has colourful feathers all over her back,
She flies through the sky as quick as a bat,
Flappity-flappity-flappity-flap.

Squawkity-squawkity-squawkity-squawk,
The parrot loves to talk, talk and talk,
Some are colourful and some are not,
Squawkity-squawkity-squawkity-squawk.

Charlotte Rawlings (7)
Wellsprings Primary School, Taunton

The Dinosaur's Life

Chompity-stompity-chompity-stomp
The dinosaur has a gigantic lunch
Some dinosaurs are humungous
And some are tincy wincy
Chompity-stompity-chompity-stomp

Groaning-moaning-groaning-moaning
The dinosaur is sadly alone
Sometimes roaring, sometimes snoring
Groaning-moaning-groaning-moaning

Chompity-stompity-chompity-stomp
The dinosaur has a gigantic lunch
Some dinosaurs are humungous
and some are tincy wincy
Chompity-stompity-chompity-stomp.

Tianna Frances Hathaway (8)
Wellsprings Primary School, Taunton

The Triceratops

Chompity-chompity-chompity-chomp,
The triceratops munches with a bomp.
Some dinosaurs are plant-eaters and
some eat meat,
Chompity-chompity-chompity-chomp.

Stampity-stampity-stampity-stamp,
The triceratops walks with a plomp.
Some dinosaurs are loud and some are not,
Stampity-stampity-stampity-stamp.

Chompity-chompity-chompity-chomp,
The triceratops munches with a bomp.
Some dinosaurs are plant-eaters and
some eat meat,
Chompity-chompity-chompity-chomp.

Jared Smale (8)
Wellsprings Primary School, Taunton

The Dog

Howledy-howledy-howledy-howl,
The dog's favourite thing is to howl, howl, howl.
Some dogs are black and some dogs are not,
Howledy-howledy-howledy-howl.

Fluffedy-fluffedy-fluffedy-fluff,
The dog is all covered with fluffedy fur,
He is the fluffiest dog in the world,
Fluffedy, fluffedy, fluffedy, fluff.

Howledy-howledy-howledy-howl,
The dog's favourite thing is to howl, howl, howl.
Some dogs are black and some dogs are not,
Howledy-howledy-howledy-howl.

Angela Mackay (8)
Wellsprings Primary School, Taunton

The Horse

Clippity-cloppity-clippity-clop
The horse skips along with a clippty clop
Some horses are brown and some are not
Clippity-cloppity-clippity-clop.

Chompity-chimpity-chompity-chomp
The horse chomps along with a chompity chomp
Its fur is all covered with chocolatey choc
Chompity-chimpity-chompity chomp.

Clippity-cloppity-clippity-clop
The horse skips along with a clippity clop
Some horses are brown and some are not
Clippity-cloppity-clippity-clop.

Abigail Ralph (7)
Wellsprings Primary School, Taunton

The Rabbit

Hippity-hoppity-hippity-hop,
The rabbit jumps around with a flippity-flop,
Some rabbits are grey and some are choc,
Hippity-hoppity-hippity-hop.

Crunchity-crunchity-crunchity-crunch,
The rabbit is eating his carrot cake lunch,
The naughty rabbit drank all of the punch,
Crunchity-crunchity-crunchity-crunch.

Hippity-hoppity-hippity-hop,
The rabbit jumps around with a flippity-flop,
Some rabbits are grey and some are choc,
Hippity-hoppity-hippity-hop.

Alexa Harris (7)
Wellsprings Primary School, Taunton

The Pterodactyl

Flappity-floppity-flappity-flop
The pterodactyl swoops in and finds food
Some pterodactyls are black and some are not
Flappity-floppity-flappity-flop.

Washity-wishity-washity-wish
The pterodactyl loves the food he eats
Some are red and some are not
Washity-wishity-washity-wish.

Flappity-floppity-flappity-flop
The pterodactyl swoops in and finds food
Some pterodactyls are black and some are not
Flappity-floppity-flappity-flop.

Mia Squire (7)
Wellsprings Primary School, Taunton

The Rabbit

Hippity-hoppity-hippity-hop
The rabbit's ears go flippity flop
Some rabbits are black and some rabbits are not
Hippity-hoppity-hippity-hop.

Crunchity-crunchity-crunchity-crunch
The rabbit crunches his carrot for lunch
Juicy and crunchy, all orange delight
Crunchity-crunchity-crunchity-crunch.

Hippity-hoppity-hippity-hop
The rabbit's ears go flippity flop
Some rabbits are black and some rabbits are not
Hippity-hoppity-hippity-hop.

Emily Cross (7)
Wellsprings Primary School, Taunton

The Crocodile

Swampity-swampity-swampity-swamp
The crocodile has a romp through the swamp
Some crocs are hungry and some crocs are rude
Swampity-swampity-swampity-swamp.

Lumpity-bumpity-lumpity-back
The croc's jaws go snappity-snap
Some green scales doing some laps
Lumpity-bumpity-lamity-back.

Swampity-swampity-swampity-swamp
The crocodile has a romp through the swamp
Some crocs are hungry and some crocs are rude
Swampity-swampity-swampity-swamp.

Lewis Horrobin (8)
Wellsprings Primary School, Taunton

The Tiger

Roaridy-roaridy-roaridy-roar,
There goes a tiger with a ferocious jaw,
Some tigers bite and some use claws,
Roaridy-roaridy-roaridy-roar.

Swiggaldy-swaggaldy-swiggaldy-sway,
The tiger walks around with some swiggaldy sway,
The tiger has a picture of him on a flag,
Wiggaldy-swaggaldy, swiggaldy, swag.

Roaridy-roaridy-roaridy-roar,
There goes a tiger with a ferocious jaw,
Some tigers bite and some use claws,
Roaridy-roaridy-roaridy-roar.

Thomas Harriss (7)
Wellsprings Primary School, Taunton

The Dinosaurs

Chompity-stompity-chompity-stomp
The dinosaurs go chomp, chomp, chomp
Some dinosaurs are vicious and some are not
Chompity-stompity-chompity-stomp.

Bitety-gulpity-bitety-gulp
The dinosaur bites you down in one gulp
Some dinosaurs are herbivores and some are not
Bitety-gulpity-bitety-gulp.

Chompity-stompity-chompity-stomp
The dinosaurs go chomp, chomp, chomp
Some dinosaurs are vicious and some are not
Chompity-stompity-chompity-stomp.

Ollie Webber (8)
Wellsprings Primary School, Taunton

The Puppy

Wiggity-waggity-wiggity-wag,
The puppy runs round in a ziggity-zag,
He really enjoys playing games of tag,
Wiggity-waggity-wiggity-wag.

Barkity-barkity-barkity-bark,
The puppy is noisy when he goes to the park,
Sometimes he is scared of the dark,
Barkity-barkity-barkity-bark.

Wiggity-waggity-wiggity-wag,
The puppy runs round in a ziggity-zag,
He really enjoys playing games of tag,
Wiggity-waggity-wiggity-wag.

Alesha James (7)
Wellsprings Primary School, Taunton

The Spinosaurus

Speedity-sprintity-speedity-sprint,
The spinosaurus goes rompity romp,
Some spinos are fast and some are not,
Speedity-sprintity-speedity-sprint.

Rumpity-rumping-rumpity-rump,
The spinosaurus goes chomping chomp,
The spinosaurus goes rampity rimp,
Rumpity-rumping-rumpity-rump.

Speedity-sprintity-speedity-sprint,
The spinosaurus goes rompity romp,
Some spinos are fast and some are not,
Speedity-sprintity-speedity-sprint.

Joshua Edward Comer (8)
Wellsprings Primary School, Taunton

The Dog

Barkity-backity-barkity-bark,
The dog went to the slippery, sloppery park.
Some dogs are light, some dogs are dark,
Barkity-backity-bark.

Woofidy-waffidy-woofidy-woof,
The dog's bark is as loud as a mark.
She walks with a pickity-pok,
Woofidy-waffidy-woofidy-woof.

Barkity-backity-barkity-bark,
The dog went to the slippery, sloppery park.
Some dogs are light, some dogs are dark,
Barkity-backity-barkity-bark.

Megan Chapman (8)
Wellsprings Primary School, Taunton

The T-Rex

Crunch-bunch-crunch-bones
The T-rex groans when he roams
He roars when he pours his supper into his mouth
Crunch-bunch-crunch-bones

Crash-bash-crash-smash
The T-rex has the power of a tall tower
His tail is like a whip when he strikes his prey
Crash-bash-crash-smash

Crunch-bunch-crunch-bones
The T-rex groans when he roams
He roars when he pours his supper into his mouth
Crunch-bunch-crunch-bones.

Elliot Barr (8)
Wellsprings Primary School, Taunton

The T-Rex

Stompity-rompty-dompity-chompity,
He roars and snaps and loves his lunch,
He does not want to lose his lunch,
Stompity-rompty-dompity-chompity.

Squashing-munching-crushing-bashing,
He loves to eat smaller animals than him,
Squashing-munching-crushing-bashing.

Stompity-rompty-dompity-chompity,
He roars and snaps and loves his lunch,
He does not want to lose his lunch,
Stompity-rompty-dompity-chompity.

Rosie Lynne Tiffany (7)
Wellsprings Primary School, Taunton

The T-Rex

Stompedy-wompety-stompedy-stomp
A big T-rex stomping through the swamp
Some are big, some are not
Stompedy-stomp-stomp

Chompedy-stompety-lompety-stomp
A big T-rex having his lunch
Chomping away, fierce and fearless
Bigger than the rest
Fompe-fomp-womp.

Stompedy-wompety-stomp
A big T-rex stomping through the swamp
Some are big, some are not
Stompedy-stomp-stomp.

Hollie Jarman (8)
Wellsprings Primary School, Taunton

T-Rex

Hopity-hipity-jumpity-scare
The T-rex roars a great scare
Some are little and some are ginormous
Hopity-hipity-jumpity-scare.

Stompity-rompity-rompity-stomp
The dinosaur goes chomp, chomp, chomp
Some are good and some are not
Stompity-rompity-rompity-stomp.

Hopity-hipity-jumpity-scare
The T-rex roars a great scare
Some are little and some are ginormous
Hopity-hipity-jumpity-scare.

Mason Le Prevost (7)
Wellsprings Primary School, Taunton

The Diplodocus

Crunch-munch-crunch-munch
The dinos have a vegetarian lunch
Dippy is strong and Dippy is tall
Crunch-munch-crunch-munch.

Bunch-crunch-bunch-crunch
Dippy's strength is as strong as an ox
Some dinos are small and some are tall
Bunch-crunch-bunch-crunch.

Crunch-munch-crunch-munch
The dinos have a vegetarian lunch
Dippy is strong and Dippy is tall
Crunch-munch-crunch-munch.

Noah Derbe (7)
Wellsprings Primary School, Taunton

T-Rex

Hunch-munch-hunch-munch
The T-rex eats with a crunch
Some T-rex are green and some are mean
Hunch-munch-hunch-munch.

Roar-jaw-boar-caw
The T-rex makes the ground rumble with his roar
Some dinos are loud and some are proud
Roar-jaw-boar-claw.

Hunch-munch-hunch-munch
The T-rex eats with a crunch
Some T-rex are green and some are mean
Hunch-munch-hunch-munch.

Richard Continho Leitao (7)
Wellsprings Primary School, Taunton

The Tyrannosaurus Rex

Choppity-woppity-womp
The tyrannosaurus, roar, roar, roar
Some eat dead meat, some don't
Choppity-woppity-womp

Crunch-munch-crunch-munch
The T-rex loves dead meat for lunch.
Crunch-munch-crunch-munch

Choppity-woppity-womp
The tyrannosaurus, roar, roar, roar
Some eat dead meat, some don't
Choppity-woppity-womp.

Theo Richie Hind (7)
Wellsprings Primary School, Taunton

The Pig

Oinkity, oinkity, oinkity, oink
The pig has a roll and a roll in the mud
Some pigs are pink and some pigs are spotty
Oinkity, oinkity, oinkity, oink.

Chompity, chompity, chompity, chomp
The pig eats apples with a chompity chomp.

Harry Woodland (8)
Wellsprings Primary School, Taunton

Unicorn Magic Land

Unicorns dancing, unicorns prancing, one with a red beret,
Elephants swaying, elephants praying, one with a bright red bow.
These are the creatures of Unicorn Magic Land.
All animals welcome to join our band.
The giraffe is playing the saxophone while the lizard is on the trombone,
The tiger is blowing the cornet and the snake got stung by a hornet.
Now to say our goodbyes, we will see you all soon,
Meet us on the moon.
Greetings from Unicorn Magic Land.

Kacey Connolly (9)
Westonbirt Prep School, Tetbury

Young Writers

YOUNG WRITERS INFORMATION

We hope you have enjoyed reading this book – and that you will continue to in the coming years.

If you're a young writer who enjoys reading and creative writing, or the parent of an enthusiastic poet or story writer, do visit our website **www.youngwriters.co.uk**. Here you will find free competitions, workshops and games, as well as recommended reads, a poetry glossary and our blog.

If you would like to order further copies of this book, or any of our other titles, then please give us a call or visit **www.youngwriters.co.uk**.

Young Writers
Remus House
Coltsfoot Drive
Peterborough
PE2 9BF
(01733) 890066
info@youngwriters.co.uk